THREADS OF GOLD

THREADS OF GOLD

Poems by Ric Giardina

Photographs by Barbara Murray

Willow
ISLE PRESS

Willow Isle Press
16190 Harwood Road
Los Gatos, CA 95032

Some of these poems have previously appeared in magazines,
newspapers, newsletters, journals, and anthologies, including

Emerging from Invisibility
Courageous Journeys
Parents in Love
The San Jose Mercury News
Voices

Library of Congress Card Number 99-67035
ISBN 1-892193-03-5

Cover and text design by Bill Turner
Typography by TBH Typecast, Inc.
Printed cooperatively with Patchwork Press

FIRST EDITION

This book is for my wife,
Betsy,
who has given me more gifts of love than any one man deserves,
including our daughter,
Annalisa,
who has brought her own gifts of love
and to whom this book is also dedicated.

ACKNOWLEGEMENTS

First and foremost, heartfelt thanks to Barbara Murray for the sharing of her photographic art; for the many hours spent sitting under the willow tree while I read her my poems and she envisioned photographs that reflected her responses; for the countless days of shooting, developing, accepting or rejecting, and shooting again; and for her love and support.

Special thanks to Susan J. Sparrow for her professional and personal guidance to make this book a reality, for steering the course from the poems in my heart to the book in your hands, and for just being a great friend.

My gratitude to Hal Zina Bennett who has been a guiding force and personal mentor in my life as a writer since Barbara Murray dragged me to hear him speak at the Unity Church in Walnut Creek years ago. His experience, encouragement and love have been freely given since that first day.

And, lastly, special thanks to Mary Ann Tyson who frequently held the light aloft while I looked for the keys to my life.

Bless you all!

Ric

I would like to express my gratitude to my parents and siblings for their encouragement as I continually climbed out onto the skinny branches; to BBT for the never-ending adventure in fun; to my sons, Robert and David, who hold my heart; and to Bud who thought all things were possible and to John who proved it was true.

Barbara

CONTENTS

1
Tightly Woven Threads

2
Spiritual Threads

3
Distant Threads

4
Threadbare

1 | *Tightly Woven Threads*

Carmela

What happened that you went away?
What caused a rift too deep to try to cross?
What did I do or fail to do that pains you still so deeply
That we cannot stand face-to-face today?

Carmela, mother, frightened girl, who as a child now had one,
Unready for the role, afraid, no doubt, your girlish dreams were over,
Not there for me, nor I for you, but what can be expected of the child
Who has no light to guide him?
      God! I'm sorry.

Afraid. All those years afraid. I learned my strength and self-sufficiency
      And more.
            I learned to build a wall. A life of brick and stone
            To fend off all the hurt of feeling.
      But nothing
            Could prepare me for the pain of feeling once again.

The aching doesn't stop, but ticks away the seconds into hours into days and years.
A score of years, Carmela!
      How much more before we make our peace?
           Or I make mine?
What do you want?
      What have you wanted all this time?
           I thought at times I knew, but I was always wrong.
Or was I?

Was the game for you to play the one who's never satisfied?
      Who's always wronged, surviving pain,
           The martyr in a world in which
I play the callous and uncaring son?
      Was that the game?
           And did I lose?
              Or you?
           Or did we both?

The Wife of the Fisherman

My mother's dreams were never quite enough for her
She dreamed once of a house
       in lush suburbia
       and this she did achieve,
But it was not enough
And did not make her happy.

She dreamed then of a large sedan
Its sleek design enough
       to cause the neighbors' envy,
And this, too, made its way to her
       in its own time,
But it was not enough
And did not make her happy.

She wanted, too, to visit paradise before she died
To walk across its crystal sands and swim its azure seas,
And better than a single trip, she went there many times,
And finally made her home there.
The balance of her life was spent
       among its fragrant flowers and soaring palms,
But somehow even this,
       this ultimate of all her dreams,
       was not enough
And did not make her happy.

And so it was with every gift she asked for and received.
The thing in hand was never quite as satisfying
       as the thought of having it had been.
And I believe that near the end of life,
The realization may have struck her of the waste
  The years spent yearning and not being,
       decades of asking and not giving thanks
And I think she gave up, thinking this was all there was to life
       and it was not enough
       and would not make her happy.

I'd like to think this lesson is not lost on me.
In viewing my own life, I see the times I've done the same
Requested, prayed, even beseeched for some event or gift
To make its way onto my path while thinking, This is it!
Only then to find the next thing more alluring
        And the next.
        And how much more beyond?
How much will be enough?
How much to make me happy?

I've not succeeded yet in quenching these desires,
But I have learned, at least, that gratitude for
  what I have,
        and who I'm with
        and who loves me
        and those I love
Does much to calm this tendency to turn away
        from gifts received
        to see what will be next.
And this, I think, will be enough
        and may be all it takes
        to make me happy.

My Mother Died Today

My mother died today.
There should be tears, but I have none. You see,
For me, she died too many years ago
To feel the pain again today.

I know there must have been a time when she held me,
Loved me, looked at my infant's face with gladness saying,
"My son!" But I remember none of this. Instead,
My memories of her live in worlds of anger and of hurt.
Both hers and mine. Then nothing for too many years.

With risk, I called my father just to tell him of my sadness for him losing his life's partner.
      He did not want to hear from me.
"I'll come to see her and see you," I said, in hopes of healing all our pasts.
    "Don't come," he said. "She didn't want you here. She told me so."
      "Don't come," my brother said.
        "Don't come," my brother's wife.
   And so I've stayed away and chosen not to go.
    For her.
      For them.
        But, most of all, for me.

Strange. Somehow, through this all, there is a softness in my heart
    Around the thought of her that I have never felt before this time.
Perhaps it is that letting go her body and dropping for the first the masks that separated us
    through life,
We can, for once, share who we are at depth.
    Without judgment,
      Without demands,
        Without the pain that nagged her life and mine.

My mother died today. There should be tears, but I have none.

My Brother

My brother could not see the crime in not living every day.
He didn't seem to know that waiting for his good to come
Like a spider with no web would gain him little in the end.
And, yet, he waited far too long, as though this was his only option.

My brother has his handicaps and these have served him well.
One cannot speak to him of things too sensitive, too true;
The stress is great on him and he is seized and cannot hear or speak.
And thus, the weight is great on us who would so speak to him
And tell him what we think he needs to hear or what we need to say.

Our parents' hopes were that their boys would accomplish many things.
In youth, he was the star. An athlete, popular with boys, and favored
By the girls at school. Boyish, handsome, tall, and dark, he'd win your
Heart as no one else I ever knew. But, like some hidden and recurring Hyde,
There was this part to him too wild, untamed, and bent on pushing hard
On every rule and every one who held him up for measure or to task.

And it was this that finally calmed him, but too much. Escaping
From a life perceived as strangling, the car he rode in wrecked,
And with it much of his planned future. The guilt has survived best,
Both his and theirs. And mine as well. As each of us, for years,
Has tried to find some order in this changed and painful circumstance.

For Mary Ann

Walking to see her
>through the wreckage
>>the storm has wrought.

Fallen branches mar the path with beauty,
>Making me aware of where I step
>And that I step

Toward questions
>Perhaps The Question
>which may lead me to the conversation
>that will recreate my life.

My Father, Then

A painful man, my father.
He views the world though squinted eyes
    which let in just the light to see
    what he's determined is already there.
No peace for such a man nor for those who live within his sphere.

We've tried to talk.
But every conversation leads no place but to the past.
    The land of blame and tortured words
    where nothing means what was intended
    and no intended meaning can survive.
A bleak and wretched place that past.

My father sees the world
    in black and white like silent films
    in which the rest of us are actors,
    gagged by his device and to whose every act and look
    he adds his own offensive dialogue.
The offense is to him of course; his actions never would offend.

He views himself the righteous one,
    who's never sinned,
    reminding us at every turn
    how much he has forgiven,
    though, he says, in sharp retort
    he never can forget.
And in this world he lives with those of us who seek to love him.

My Father, Now

The man has changed,
Removed the shackles on the box
That covered all his heart.
And changed.

And now, expanding, that heart throbs with love
And a lifetime worth of unexpressed desire to be loved.
One cannot help but wonder what it was
That struck him such a blow
That he could live life so constrained
For years becoming decades.
And then, what shock or force could set him on the path
To reconciliation, joy, and love,
And open up his heart to now accept the gifts
So many held in readiness for him?

And now, if any pain I see,
His eyes reflect the sorrow of regret
For luscious moments cast aside
When they were ripe and begging to be savored.
I see the pain for time he views as lost,
And all the could-have-beens that never are to be.
But do not be mistaken: Any pain in him
Only mirrors that within my heart.

What comfort I can give to him and he to me
Consists of living now as though our pasts,
Both lived together and apart, did not exist.
In truth, there's only now. Right now.
And having that, if only for another day,
Such as it is, is fair exchange
For dealing with the phantom of the pain
We both believed we suffered.

The New Life

The bloom of youth is in her cheeks
   despite her years,
And his white hair and cragged face
   belie the young man of his heart.
They came from different places,
   Yet the same,
And carried to their time of meeting
   kindred life events
     A full, long married life
      that had its pain
      and its rewards,
    Their children grown,
    A move to nature's paradise,
    A death for each,
    The fear
      and loneliness
       that come with such a parting,
    A quiet time of solitude,
 And then
   New freedom found
   To try a new beginning
    Reaching out
    Exploring
    Sharing
    Finding someone new
   Using blocks of time called days
   to build a new and shining life.

Now they come together, here,
This bride and groom of decades
   To join their hands
   To seal their hearts.
At this late time in life
   a gift of Hope
   an act of Faith in God's immortal Love
A lesson for us all to live each day
   as though it is the only one.

To honor this,
> their friends and family
> crossed a continent
> and sea

To be with them
> amongst God's Love
> as it's presented here

To be with them
> and wish them well
> on this,
> the very first day
> of their new life together.

Frances Weeks

Quietly she came into my life. And quietly she left.
Who could have thought the wife of just another short-term boss
      Would fill a place that's lasted half my life?
            I can't remember
                  Our first meeting at their home when I came once with David
                  To finish up some project that had taken us the day and now
                  Would take up more that evening.
She made us dinner while we worked.
      That was in 1970, though now it seems she's always been
            Somewhere in the background
                Long before we met
                    Like some dear guardian angel.
I had just finished college and in the fall would start law school.
      Somewhere in that crack she fell into my life and I in hers,
            And I am not the same nor want to be.

She was an older woman, older even than her husband, David. He,
Whom I always did respect and grew in time to love.
      But Frances, even then somewhere in her sixties,
            Was someone special from the first.
      Just the knowing of her placed me somehow closer to all Truth.
      She was an easy one to love. An easy one to be with.

There always was a playful tone to everything she did or said,
      To every look she gave.
      "Oh Gawd!" she'd say in that Down Eastern accent from her native Maine.
      "Oh Gawd!" when something unbelievable had happened or
            When something funny or too tragic entwined our lives.
      But always, always with a reassuring twinkle in her eye.
      That twinkle let you know that everything would be all right.
          No.
      Let you know that everything was now all right and would so stay.
      She knew. She always knew the Truth.

The years passed. I matured and changed, but Frances never changed.
Perfect as she was, content, relaxed and pleased with what life gave her.
       All the little tasks that filled her day.
I lived with her and David twice for several months
       When army training brought me near their home.
       Virginia in the winter moving into spring it was both times.
               Years later
       When I visited, my wife and new child in my tow,
       There never was a question of acceptance.

Frances came to me one day to simply say
               How pleased they were about my choice,
                   About my wife,
                       About my child.
       My family did not do that. Perhaps could not do that. But Frances could.

For nearly twenty-seven years our Frances kept in touch.
       And we with them.
Each Christmas came a box with items bought, but mostly made by
Frances' hands. Ornaments that have and will adorn our tree each year.
       Simple things.
               Little things.
                   Brimming with love. And items
       Made or purchased for a little girl she rarely saw but clearly loved.

And she would write of her life as she aged.
       Of David's authored books
               Of visitors who came and went
                   Of storms that wreaked some damage
                   To their cottage on the beach.
And always it was she who wrote to send us greetings and the news.
       That's how we knew.
               The printed return label held just David's name
               As if to warn us of its contents.
       We knew, somehow we knew, from only that
               For it was always she who wrote.
"Frances died on January 17th," his note began.
       He told us of the circumstances.
               Quick.
                   No notice.
                       Nothing long.
       A soul deciding to move on and taking it in stride. As Frances was in life.

And now there is a place, an empty place in life for me where once
The thought of Frances at her home had lived.
      I can no longer call her just to see how she and David are.
      I will no longer hear her voice
            Encouraging, accepting, sharing little joys that are to be.
      No mail will come from her with news.
      No box of handmade Christmas gifts. And yet
            Her gentleness is with me still and always will remain.
      She was
            And is
                        An inspiration in her quiet love of life
                        And how she was with those whose paths crossed hers.

She taught me much, this woman from the very north of Maine.
Much more than she could ever know, although I tried to tell her many times
      Of what she meant to me. And David, too.

Yes, quietly she came into my life.
      And quietly she left.
            But left me for that different than before.
            And much the better.

If All I Had Were You

If all I had were you, would be enough
To get me through each day
And bring me home again to where
Your glow would warm me to my heart.

If all I had were you, would be enough
To have the sun shine for me
Through those bright blue eyes
And I would know God's love.

If all I had were you, would be enough
To ease the stress of life.
My soul would have no torments,
Resting easy in its journey.

Sometimes I feel alone, abused by life,
I think of what I'd have if all I had were you,
And know that it would be enough.
And gratitude and love are all I feel,
For it is so that I have you.

To Betsy

You tend our child with love. With grace
So pure, the angels stand amazed, attendant
As they are on God. No day triumphant
Yet every day a triumph in itself.

Though worlds apart, adult and child,
Each day some new mature awareness,
Placed there by you, glows in her unfledged eyes,
Just as in you each day with her your Child awakes.

What special gifts you bring to her! To me,
In seeing you and her and you in her. A thousand-fold
My love for you has grown since we were just we two
And thought to share our love with someone yet unknown.

My heart is full. With love for you. For her. For us.
That we, together, did create this miracle she is.

In April Come the Roses

In April come the roses to her native California. Born here
Just nine short years ago at this same time,
       She blossoms forth
       As full of promise as the month in which she came.

This land is equally a part of her as she is part of it.
Her blue eyes sparkle as the arching sky that sees
No rain for half a year beginning now
As if in honor of her birth month.

The golden sun.
       The golden sand. Reflections
          Of her glistening hair which
          Wavy, long, is full of life.
             Just as she is.

A warm and wondrous winter's day a year ago.
I watch as she runs wild along the beach
       Zigzagging back and forth
       Where ocean meets the land.
Her joy is unrestrained. A water sprite,
This girl of eight dry summers seems.

And in her step and in her joy I see myself,
       Not only in the past,
       But as I am within,
       Now seen without.

Her gift is the expression of the joy I feel inside.
This is the gift she offers all.
       But even this,
       Much as it is, is only promise.
          All there is is yet to be.
Just as the April roses, ambrosial as they are
In beauty and in fragrance for us winter wearied folk,
Turn out to be precursors, meager messengers
Proclaiming scanty doses of the summer soon to come.

Threads of Gold

My daughter still adores me.
I've heard other fathers say
"Oh, yes, She's at that age,
But wait, she's still quite young
And adolescence still a far way off."
I think they think we do not talk
And have no disagreements.
That we live in some fairy tale
Which, like some video, someday will end.
Instead, I see my daughter grow each day,
Her womanhood takes shape before my eyes.
We grow apart, yes. This is natural
And so necessary for her sense of self,
But something still connects us.
Threads of gold from her heart to my own,
And these can never break.

2 | *Spiritual Threads*

Past Present

The past bleeds forth its image on today. It matters not
If that time was one of joy or sorrow, the past is still
A thief that steals away the treasure of the now
And has us live a life that isn't real, that is not true.

A myriad of visions from the past scream out. Declaring
Who was right and who was wrong. Demanding retribution
For a wound received. Suggesting guilt as salve to ease the pain
Of having hurt another. A most demanding mistress is the past.

Where are we when we listen? We are not here in time,
Nor are we there. The there of then is gone as steam
Which dissipates and joins the greater fabric of the world,
Combining with the clouds, and rain, and rivers and the sea.

Just so, our past should have no presence in the now,
Although it's brought us to this place in time. The skein
Is added to the textile of our lives and can be touched
For joy of memory and sensation. But never lived again.

Redemption

One knows not from where comes redemption,
But come to us it will
And come to us it must.
  Perhaps in just the glint of light on a petal's satin skin,
  Or in the smile or frown of friend or foe,
  Or in the way a shadow leaves a trail of sadness,
  Or the giggle of a child's unbridled joy.

Somehow, yes, it comes.
For we are, each of us, predestined by our higher selves
To find our way to God.
It is the place our journey first begins.
That singleness, the One. But One can simply be. It is.
  It cannot run along a brook,
    Or smell a fragrant flower
      Or see the endless sky
        Or share its Love
For none of this there is in One, yet all of this there be.
The paradox is great. And True.

So we came off apart from One to be detached, as if we could.
To separate to sense and see and hear and taste and smell
The pleasures and the pain. The wealth of all experience.

And somehow in that coming off, we came sometime to think
That we were separate from the Power and the Love of One,
But it resides within and can be triggered by some act,
  or vision
    or some thought
      or sound.
And we call this redemption.

Commitment

To some, commitment seems an iron mantle that would so
Heavy weigh them down, they have no will to take it up.
To some, commitment seems a shackle that chains them to the past
Excluding all the options that the future world might hold.

To some, commitment seems a rock to which they tether unknown lives;
A promise made without the knowledge as to what the promise means.
A request, nay, demand to give up all that there could be in honor of
Some shapeless thing that may not have a name and has less present meaning.

To some, commitment seems the end of all that is and also what will be.
Forced down one road while peering longingly like Lot's regretful wife
Down other roads that cannot now be journeyed. The traveler who
Loses all — the chosen road as well as all the others.

But then, to some, commitment is an open portal fearlessly
Through which they step knowing God's good sense of timeliness
And trusting that the very act of giving up oneself is what it takes
To live, to truly live in concert with themselves and, thus, with God.

Yes, to the Spirit minded, commitment is an easy thing
That flexes soft and moves with them and with their lives.
And grants their every wish and heart's desire. The engine
That empowers who they are and what they are about.

To these, commitment is the book of knowledge, which, when opened
At their will, provides them what they need to learn about themselves.
Having once been started, this book is not put down, for only at the last
Do they discover what they were to learn and how it was they learned it.

Seascape

I stand by the eternal sea
An Eternal Being.
Timeless, it measures time with waves,
Timeless, I measure mine with days.
Knowing we are one
He and I
She and I
The sea and I.
And in that Knowing
I move on in Life.

The Mission

The rip in the clouds lying dark and low
Across a landscape now steel gray
Reveals the sky of unbelievable blue beyond.

My heart, heavy with its own cloud cover,
Attempts to find a clearing somewhere
Beyond the pain that holds it hostage.

Just like the cloudless sky beyond the gray
I know a dome of joy surrounds this gloomy heart.
If only I could pierce the feelings of the moment.

It is the mission of my life at this stark point
To tell the truth, to speak authentic words,
To do all that there is that I see mine to do.

And this, this cup, shall not pass from my hand,
This pain is mine to give. This pain is mine to feel.
Right now, this is all there is to me. It is consuming.

Once passing through, the tasks complete,
The sapphire essence of God's joy awaits.
But now I am reminded only by a leaden sky
And a jagged tear of blue that mirrors my own heart.

Solitude

In the silence, alone with my thoughts
Like a deaf man
      With nothing to break
      The monologue inside my head.
That is sound to me and, now,
All the sound there is.
      The silence can be maddening.
        Deafening.
      All encompassing of attention.
I will do most anything to break
The tension that has captured me.
      Except move.
        Except speak.
When I am being wise, I only listen.

Journey

The Sacred Place is full of pain
    and painless.
The Sacred Place is cordoned off by fences
    staved with fear,
    and
    barbed with doubt
        as if the fear and doubt themselves
        like despots seeking patronage,
        know anyone who makes it to this place
        is free from paying tribute.

The Sacred Place, while hidden
    desires nothing more than to be found.
The Sacred Place is where our dreams
    are thought to go to die. Instead,
    it is the very place that hope is born anew.

The Sacred Place appears to lie at the surface of our souls,
    and seems to float there,
    seemingly so close at hand
    while we, in reaching down, can never grasp it
        with our hands or
        with our minds.
    It's only heart that makes the journey here.
    For here, compassion waits.

The Day of Peace

Peace will come upon us like a cool mist,
Circling, encompassing, surrounding us
    with light and joy and love.
Not an absence, but a presence,
    joining all of us together
And the spaces in-between.
    Between the hammer and the cartridge,
    Between the hand and what it strikes,
    Between the anger and the action.
Like the gentle breath of Heaven,
Peace will comfort every soul.

Peace will come upon us from within us,
Swirling up, escaping out, connecting us
    in ways we only dream.
Spirit rising, ever present,
    finding in us each its home
Every heart full of its presence.
    Present to the natural wonder,
    Present to the lack of danger,
    Present to the power of Love.
Like the scent of sage on soft winds
Peace will lure us to the Truth.

Peace will come upon us like warm thunder,
Breaking out, crackling light, a silent fireworks
    display of joy.
Strong and urging, unrestrained,
    burning bright to guide the way
To acquittal of our dark past.
    Past mistakes seen now as lessons,
    Past divisions viewed as whole,
    Past pain gone as never present
Like a beacon for each person,
Peace will show our world as One.

Redwood Meditation

A redwood tree grows every day
A bit. It takes its gifts from God —
The light, clear water, air and minerals
It cannot see but knows through faith are there
And builds itself anew and bit by bit.
When hot, bright sun adorns its limbs
Or cooling mountain mists and gentle rains cascade,
Not judging, it finds its path and grows
A bit each day.

One redwood tree beside my home
Was little once. Eight years ago
I strung its boughs with Christmas lights
And used no ladder or stepping stool to reach
The top where I had placed a yellow star.
With no concern that tree has grown
Until it soars some sixty feet and more
And I can only see its highest point from far away.
No lights this year.

A man in Spirit grows each day
A bit. The difference is we watch
And wait and judge each spurt of growth
And every revelation. We notice times we fail
To trust or live in faith and must remember
Not to contemplate too much their meaning.
But then, like redwood trees, we have the choice
To take our gifts from God and build ourselves anew
And bit by bit.

Sentinel's Watch

Startled by the sense of sleep, I freeze
And raise my head to look about to see
What place this is that I have come to.
Unbidden inattention, unnoticed until now,
Has brought me here to this despite my charge.

"My destiny is mine to cause!" I'd said,
And started down the worthy road.
But somewhere down the path I'd trod
I found myself alone and somehow off my course.
And see now how I'd wandered off in sleep.

Like Peter could I not keep watch the hour?
Like some small child bored with the game,
I cast aside my faith and stiff-necked set about
To find the way. The goal I sought escapes me now.
My fresh awakened state can scant recall.

As fear takes hold and starts to spread, I know
There is a choice. I could go back, expecting to regain
My now eluded purpose. Perhaps retrace my steps?
And then I see again that any path I'd choose
Would be the one that takes me to the perfect place.

No longer frozen, simply stopped, I reassess.
This momentary lapse which seemed so much a loss
Provides another byway, a different road, an altered view
That leads but to the same awareness. I've kept my watch
For part of it is to forget at times and wander without purpose.

The Gathering

The men are gathering
Coming close from far away
Hearts in hand, they gather here
To share and breathe the Light of God.

So honestly the feelings flow,
The mask each man has brought
To wear of habit is quickly tossed aside
Then thrown away in favor of his Being.

And each begins to bring about within Himself
The new world order. No hesitancy here to deal
And take a chance. The deck is stacked,
And owned by God. Each card the King of Hearts.

Las Alas del Águila

On eagles' wings the men soar high above the redwoods.
Crystal light, an effervescence of the air delights the eye
And warms the soul, providing peace to all. Seemingly,
A momentary elemental essence, but always there. If only
We would open wide our hearts to let it out and let it in.

The men on eagles' wings soar higher still. Higher
Than they ever have before. Alive. All love. Alone.
But with no loneliness for each is part of all and all are part of One.
These men have turned within and found there joy and sadness,
Hopes and tears, and for some, too, there is the lurking Fear.

The Fear will rise if we just let it take its grasp, and drag us
Down into the basest of our feelings of despair and loneliness.
The Fear will ring the mind and strangle Love and hold us
Hostage to we know not what. Frightened and yet willing then
We seize the fate that Fear provides without looking in its eye.

And some soar highest — to the very heights of God and Spirit.
These are the ones, who, fearful, even so reach in, reach down,
Reach out and pulling out the Fear, examine it and see it for the lie
It is. By doing this they change their Fear to feathers used
To build a stronger wing with longer reach to soar them higher still.

The Turning Point

The turning point takes just a moment,
Though I can see its roots in years long past.
The time had come when I must choose to be.
And not to do. And not to have.

This choice, when made, will close me off forever
From a place I never cared to be, though drawn there,
Time and time again. A single moment's clarity
    Of light.
           Of vision.
                      Certainty. Seeing how
My life has changed and knowing how that life
Will change again. But only by this choice.

How many times before came I to this same crossroads
Its landscape so disguised I noted little I can see today?
How many times that other choice?
    That subroutine,
           The loop that carries me a long, far way,
              But then returns me
Here, bedraggled, wasted, not having learned,
    But asked to choose again?

But somehow, just now, this once I see it all so clearly.
Past choices made and consequences
                            falling
                                  out
Like beads at a bazaar. In retrospect, with clarity,
I cannot fail to see what blinded me before.

Yes, this time I can see the road. The choices
    And the certainty of each result attached like light
        Bent through a prism. One and the same.

I make my choice this time with more at stake, but
With less risk, for I can see all I can see.
        For now.

3 | *Distant Threads*

Stonehenge

Stones.
        Not tumbled.
                Placed.
And in that lies their magic.
Eons past it must have been
For now there is no record of
The who or how or why.

Only stones.
        Not tumbled.
                Placed meticulously here.
Stones of wonder even now,
When we could have the same result in hours
  with our tools.

Yet this is not the reason for our fascination.
For in these stones something special lives.
The recognition of Life's energy
        By those much closer to the land than we.
Anointed stones these must have been.
        And are.

In ritualistic majesty these stones sing to us now
Of days that none of us remembers.
Known only as "Prehistory," before man wrote,
A time when men lived day to day
And had not yet begun to calibrate the cycles in the world.

Now we measure everything and to the nth degree.
        The time for light to travel distant stars.
                Nanoseconds saved on silicon chips.
                    The oceans' endless fathoms
                    Certainly not endless any more.

Perhaps this is what calls to us the loudest from the stones,
The start of man's relentless drive to survey all the world.
Responding to that call, we sense within ourselves the time
When we were part of something simple and much wiser.

From Glastonbury Tor

From Glastonbury Tor the world looks different
Than it does from far below. The wind.
It whistles in your ears and all but silences the sounds
Of men. Of women. And of progress.
Something here there is that brings you back in time.
To days when men walked on the earth
And rarely rode or traveled any speed or distance.

A more romantic time one thinks initially.
When life must have been simpler than it is today.
And things seen in the world below would bolster this.
Fat wooled sheep graze here and there.
The hills of Somerset in pastel shades.
More greens than one could have imagined.
Small waterways run everywhere. And to the north
The glint of sun upon the sea. No distance to us
In this age of transportation. Another world to those
Who first were here proclaiming this place holy.

But for all that it is not peaceful here.
       Perhaps it is the wind.
             Perhaps the height.
Or maybe just the years of fear poured on this place,
Like wax that drips from candles
Building on the waiting stones below.

On Great Pulteney Street

Sitting in the window seat. A flat on Great Pulteney Street. Wondering
What this day will bring besides the drizzle that declares itself
This morning as is has so many others. Listening to the sounds
Of gulls and guessing that their inland tour foretells a greater rain.

Two floors below, outside, the traffic moves in seeming quiet
On this Sunday morn. Perhaps this day, here too, is one of rest.
Perhaps it is too early for the tours to start, the double-decker buses
Traveling up and down to point the place where once Jane Austin trod.

And from up here I see the rooftops well. The chimney stacks all in a
Row, the slated roofs with tin, the tiny windows for the top floor flats.
And everywhere, the stone. Huge masses of sand colored stone
Carved in places. Patterns, regal pillars, strands of garland, faces.

Within two city blocks this street becomes a bridge with storefronts
On both sides, which crosses River Avon, famed even to my youth.
A place once thought too far away to ever see. Now, down the street.
A simple walk, I'll cross it as I go for breakfast rolls and sweets.

My second cup of tea. Below, two tourists pack their car to leave,
Reminding me that soon their fate will be mine, too. The woman
Looks around and up, drinking it all in before she goes. She's wise.
And I will do the same each day that I am here on Great Pulteney Street.

In Another's Garden

Sitting. In a garden. Not mine.
No hand of mine has turned this soil
Or planted seed or tended tiny plants with love,
Not watered seedlings in a draught.
No time or toil have I expended here.
I've mowed no grass and pulled no weeds
And kept no vigilant eye for snails and other pests.

And yet, this garden feels as fully mine as though I had
Done all these things and more.

A magic place, a garden.

49

Mendip Sunset

Looking west, I notice, for the first, the sun
Has slowly slipped behind a distant hill.
The sky now seems all yellow, turning gold.
The shadows in the hollows deepen green,
And grass within the meadow between the near
Stone wall and far seems all aglow as if giving
back some of the sun it took in during day.
It is not still. Afar, a raven's cry disturbs the peace
Screeching warnings to another or to me.
A few bees continue work as though the day were just begun,
And starlings dart and capture morsels in mid-flight.
This day is coming to its measured end,
A decorated multicolored final burst of energy and light.
But for all its flash, the day is ending still
And soon will come the night with its own world.

Mount Shasta

Shasta's snow reflects the light of summer.
      Shimmering.
         Glimmering.
            Hovering above the earth
            like something otherworldly.
In the folds of her draped green landscape
Shasta's rivers run
      rocky,
         fast, and clean
            and gather into lakes
            like deep, banked currency.

And here, above the lake called Siskiyou,
      a ponderosa pine tree shades the deck
      as the sun begins to move around the cabin,
      its footprint changing
      from hard and solid shaded blocks of architectured forms
      to the filtered feathering coolness
      from the pine boughs up above.
A Western Jay alights its lowest branch and eyes me warily
No sound it makes — a strange thing in itself.
I write.
He watches.
      Hopping up one branch
         and then another
            three,
               then four,
      until he passes from my sight above the roofline.

The day is hot.
To the east,
a bit of snow from Shasta's cache
has melted
and begun its journey
to the lake
that lies below.

The Seed

The Hong Kong towers rise on ruffled hills.
White obelisks commemorating man's success at commerce.
Neon's glow replaces stars that seem to have no place here.
And to the north,
      Beyond the hills,
            A dragon waits. Eager
To regain her once abducted child,
      Return it to her fold,
            And end a hundred years of economic war,
            The moneyed victor vanquished by the very law that set it free at first.
And some maintain a tsunami of fiscal death awaits beyond those hills,
But I am not so sure.
      For each has changed since once estranged. Now,
            Both adults in their own worlds, they seek conciliation.
And like a tiny mustard seed that falls upon a vast and fertile field,
That which makes this city great — its clarity and singleness of purpose —
Will not be swept away, but will, in time, sow seeds of a new nation.

Encounter

The thunder cracked the day's heat soundly,
      But closer still the thunder of the mule deer's hooves.
          So close
It startled me as I had startled him.
       I jumped.
          He leaped.
But both stopped in mid flight as though drawn
      One to the other.

Ten yards and scrub brush just between us
      I saw him stop, then turn himself.
Around a branch he craned his head, all ears and eyes
      And watched me —
          The stranger there in his wild realm —
            As I watched him and just as curious.

And thus we stared a while, until at last
      In minutes past, our thirst for vision quenched,
         He bowed his head
          As if in greeting and farewell.

And I, the novice here,
      Did just the same.
         And we both walked away,
         Apart,
            Connected in a greater peace.

Desert Perceptions

There are soft places here in this cragged desert.
Not large,
      like meadows full of glistening grass to rest the body,
But large enough to rest the eye and soul,
Which, after all, is more.
As I sit here upon a rock
      upon a mountain
            vistas every way,
The softness overwhelms me.

Mountain peaks a distant lavender and green
    are smooth as satin,
      billowing against a singleness of blue.
Creamed cotton clouds caress those peaks
    And hide, for some, their hard and sharpened spires.

And earlier I came upon a place — a canyon boxed —
    where waters,
        when it rains,
        rush down the sides
            then down a central track of tumbled stones
            all smoothed from centuries of loving storms.

It rained last night
    and I could see in my mind's eye
    the softness that there was;
    some evidence remained.
        a waterfall created there —
           and there!
                the water's course
                arrayed dried grass in parallel and combed it smooth.
  A mighty rain it must have been, for even hours later on this day,
    there are some deepened hollows in the stone
        adrift with water
        and with life.
        Small polliwogs are swimming,
        keeping time against the hot, relentless sun
        with movement of their tails.

And close at hand, upon this rock, a gentle wind caresses me
      and cools me with the currency of my own sweat,
      expended as I climbed here.

Chartreuse lichens,
      all aglow,
      defy the sun bald-faced on rocks
      like paint spilled here and there.
And in the cracks
      and in the shade of those fluorescent stones
      soft mosses grow,
      awash in watercolor pigments,
      grays
      and greens
      and greenish grays,
      each a soothing resting place for feet far tinier than mine.

Amid the scent of dusting powder sage,
      leaves soft as kittens' ears cascade on spindled stems.
      A cactus fuchsia glory sparkles like a fabric gem.
      A silken yellow butterfly bobs
      up
      and
      down
      in its approach to raid its special nectar.

Even sound is soft and gentle here.
      For hours now the sacredness has kept me dumb.
          No voices in my head or out.

Another soft and gentle gift.
Indeed.

Woods Revisited

When I was a child I would walk in the woods
      just for the feel of it
      for the sound of the trees
      and the color of leaves
      and the taste of the air.
      And sunlight, bright yellow-green
         burning through overlapping stars of many shapes,
         the veins aglow with life
         or, diamond-white in early morning dew
         or in the clarity of afternoons beyond the rain.

My eyes would taste the moist loam in the soil
      dark and damp
      on small hillocks
      on either side the path I'd trod.

My ears alert to the sound of birds
And, sometimes seeing one,
      I'd stop to watch
      while, twittering from branch to branch
      it too,
      I knew,
      was watching me.

But now the woods have quieted
And lost the colors
And the sounds
And tastes
That, as a child, so fully captured me.

And then, perhaps it is that I, myself,
      am lost
      or captured by some other thing or things
      that leave me
      blind to colors
      deaf to sounds
      and deadened to the tastes.

I must go listen, look, and taste again the beauty of the woods.

Sirens

Wet sand
makes a serpentine road
along the shore.
Higher up,
the dry sand
glows dully in the full light of the moon.

Ocean waves break
far from the shore,
and, flattening,
roll over my feet
thousands of arcs of glistening white foam.

The round moon reflects crisp
and jagged
in the retreating water,
belying the gentle mist around its sister
high in the night sky,
softened,
and glowing
with a halo of pastel colors.

It is after midnight.
I knew I must come.
I am alone,
except for cautious tamarinds
and shy sandpipers
dodging my frothy path
as I traverse the lustrous waves
that come in and recede.

I had to come.
Leaving the others,
coming out into the night.
But I keep looking back
to see if they will join me.
They do not. And
I know they will not.
This is a time and place
I must attend.
They have no need.

I walk for miles
where ocean meets the land,
the water warm.
So is the night.
So are my thoughts.

They take me back
some twenty years
and more,
full moonlit nights,
other distant shores.
My thoughts then
wondering,
guessing
what the future held.
Now I know.

This evening, too,
despite my looking back,
I need to play the game
of guessing at tomorrow,
to wonder what the future holds.

But in the end,
I know,
some different, distant shore
its road of glistening serpentine sand
lit by a full and silver moon
will tell me that as well.

Langdale Gardens

It took me several hours to find these old apartment houses.
Nearly forty years have passed since I was here.
        And only twelve when I last saw this place.
But find it finally I did and it surprised me greatly.
Somehow, in my mind's eye it had fallen into dereliction
        And to ruins.
                Falling all apart.
                        An old abandoned shell, perhaps gone.
Replaced by some new structure,
        Even that, perhaps, already old,
        Decayed by now to some extent.

But I was not prepared for what I saw.
        Neat, white-washed brick and
        Newly painted, shiny black colonial shutters,
        Glistening white enameled trim.
        And curved wrought iron balustrades on porches showing slated steps.
        The tall encompassing shrubbery where we hid as children all now gone,
        Replaced by tiny gardens filled with flowers on this bright May day,
        Azaleas, rhododendrons, roses, all in bloom, vivid color here and there,
        And lawns, green velvet postage stamps all thick and lush and clearly
        In a gardener's gentle care.
How different from the home I knew as preteen boy
And dweller on the outer edge of the City of New York.

I walk about and find some evidence of age and the decay I had expected.
        The courtyard that my second story bedroom window overlooked,
        The very place my mother once had thrown my clothes
        When I had left them once too often on the floor,
        Looked somehow strange and alien but also yet familiar.
        The cars parked there seemed out of place and yet not so.
        With time, remembering that once here stood a row of brick garages
        For the privileged few who anted up the extra sums to shield
        Their 1950's cars the size of boats from New York's cold and heat.
        But now they all were gone.
                I could still see the remnants:
                Brick foundations all around the edge.
                And walking on.
                        In the next courtyard, as though as proof,
                        A row of old garages stood,
                        Bricks crumbling,
                        Front faces held in place by strong, long wooden beams.

As I stroll this quiet landscape I see people sitting out
    On tiny porches,
    Or on the edges of the stamp-sized lawns,
    Green and white vinyl woven chairs
    Brought down or out from tiny apartments.
They sit enjoying sunshine
And the talk of lives here on this May day,
    But I cannot remember doing this.
    The peace is palpable.
    Was it so then?
    Could it be that I could not feel it?
    Or was it real to me then,
    Long ago,
    And I have just forgotten?
    Or is it something new,
    Arrived here in this place now all refreshed with shutters,
    Balustrades and paint?

I do not know, but deep within my heart is sad,
    Yet happy, too.
    For the ones who live here.
        Now.

Mountain
Paradox

Sitting up here
the world looks
smaller than it is.
The few buildings
in this sparse landscape
stand tiny, white —
one domed,
convincing me,
a giant,
that I look upon
a miniature display
of someone's handiwork.
And so it is.

Sitting up here
the world looks
larger than it is.
The vastness of the
mountain range I see
and the shadow
of another one beyond
and beyond that
and that
convincing me the land
goes on and on
without a limit,
without an end.
And so it is.

4 | *Threadbare*

The Leave Taking

The man looked back, his body, sagged in sadness, turning.
Early morning light, gray and damp, draped itself around him
A shroud of simple, daily sadness as he looked to see
If she was looking back as well to see him as he went.

The sign was gaily painted, bright with yellow, blue, and red.
"Best Start PreSchool" it said, as though to push away
His fears and give him absolution. And in some way it did,
For they had chosen well this place they left their child each day.

And yet there was no joy in leaving her. His wife must go
To her routine an hour before him, and so to him it fell each day
To take the focus of their life and leave her at a stranger's door,
Like some repeating version of a modern fairy tale.

Not knowing what the day would bring for her, both of them
Would miss the joys and fears that came her way while
Others wiped her tears and kissed the tiny bruises as she learned.
He could not face how much they missed. They had no choice.

Yet every morning he must face it still. This task was his.
His wife, he noted with both envy and with gladness
Drew the straw by circumstance that let her drive each day
To where that eager, tiny face was waiting, just for her to come.

But for him every morning was the same. The hurried ready-making
To get her to her place so he could get to his. That moment of
Exquisite sadness as they parted at the door, his turn to walk away,
His head and heart full, knowing it would pass as his day busied him.

His eyes refocused from his mind, and he looked out again
To see her one last time before his day would capture him
And hold him in its grasp. He saw her, not engaged, but looking
Through the window after him, to see if he would see her one last time.

On Failure

In the loneliness of seeming failure, a finger
Crook'd in welcome beckons me
To view my life a series of events
Each a loss which leads no where but to the next
Connected dots that sketch a life defeated.

At times I have accepted this invite,
Willingly attending, going in, dragged down,
Thus beaten into sleep by my desires.
The harder then to wake and know the gifts
That God provides in times like these.

But more and more I see ahead to hindsight,
In seeming failure not dragged down, defeated.
Alert instead with expectation and awake to view
The present as the past, paths not to be tread, but trodden
And seeing where this road will lead, has led.

Reflections

The plane delayed. This time a gift
To meditate or contemplate.
I see my life.
                What I have done.
                        Those things I've not.
And wonder.
                What would my life be had I chosen different roads?
                Stayed on another path?

There was a time, this life, I danced and sang
                and hoped to see my name in lights
                        or on a screen
                        and on so many lips.

And earlier, I'd thought the place for me was in the Church
                Another nameless priest or monk, black-robed
                and adding to the prayers poured forth from earth to heaven.

But others had their plans for me as well
                which kept me for some time from seeing my heart's aim
                and choosing for myself which avenue to take.
                But even that was of some use.
                        It took great courage to say,
                        No.
                        And then select the thing I felt I wanted next the most.
Now,
        I see that the only paths I could have chosen
        Would have brought me here.

Exactly here.

Adobe Porch Impressions

Sitting on the porch
      The rocking chair supports me to and fro,
The old adobe building at my back
      Its windows leaking sounds of life within.
And to and fro the others pass.
      Sometimes alone.
            Sometimes in pairs.
            Or more.

Their conversation fragments rise and fall,
      Like nature's sounds upon the wind.
The voices carry much. Much more than words
      Or thoughts
            Or visions.

These are not sounds of crowds and streets
      Monotonous cacophony of cities
            Each sound distinct and shrill,
                  Attention-grabbing for the moment.

These are the sounds, instead, of Life,
      Of Love
            Of Hope
                Of Fear
                    Of Being.
A sharing here of those who came to find themselves
      And found, instead, themselves in every other.

This talk is gentle
      Shared from hearts in search of love,
            But knowing love itself's the searcher.
And even those who pass in silence share
      Acknowledged recognition:
            We are one.
            The seeker and the sought.
            And we are not alone.

The Author

I cannot sleep.
        I don't know why.
                It's three a.m.
My mind is full of images that flash. Then linger.
        Turning each one over many times before another
                Catches my attention.
Flash!
        Each pulls me elsewhere. Every way but sleep.
        The one thing that eludes me.

Tired body. Full awake. Moving, turning cautiously
Afraid to wake my wife who sleeps so quietly beside me.
The images continue.
        This to do.
                That already done.
                      Things that were forgotten.
        And hopeful things that simply will not be.
Sleep eludes me still.

Perhaps, I say, if I arise and jot down
Just these lines, my mind will calm and I can sleep.
For now.
        My thoughts begin a poem, which, having once intruded
Rolls around my head like marbles on a large tin tray.
        They cause no pain,
                But Oh!   The noise!
        The only antidote I know that works will be to write,
        To get the marbles out and down
        And somehow real on paper.
This calms them here within and halts
        the rolling   back
                    and
            forth.
And doing so permits me once again to sleep.

Bullies

The bully tore his mouth apart and sneered a snarling smile.
"Be afraid!" assailing eyes said. "Be afraid!"
And inside me some terror struck a chord that sagged my spirit.
Then like some gift I took the offered fear as mine
For it would save me from the pain of confrontation.

And this has happened many times throughout my life:
As little boy with bullies in the school yard;
As student with a teacher unwilling to be questioned;
An army sergeant and a church whose only tools were fear.

Most recently, a manager who could not understand my ways
And found himself in some way threatened. He tried instead
To force me to his will with fear. Until that time, I nearly
Always caved, accepting others' fear as mine and making it my own.

No more. I pushed back — hard. Refused acceptance of his fear
With angry love and said I would not play. He backed down
And left an opening, a space for me to be just as I am.
He didn't like the keeping of his fear. But better him than me,
For, after all, it was his fear not mine.

Reconciliation

Sometimes
it takes the pain of someone's death or
the loss of our own dream and
the anguish of thinking what might have been
to reconnect the hearts of the estranged.

Sometimes
it takes the breaking of the mirror
reflecting lives so out of phase
that neither one can see
reflections of the other in its glass.

Sometimes
it takes the telling of the truths
that never can be told and
giving voice to feelings harbored
long and hard and hurting in the breast.

Sometimes
it takes the welcoming of memory loss
that comes with getting old
and giving to its madness the hospitality
of heart and mind as though it were a gift.

Sometimes
it takes as little as a sign from heaven
hurtling itself across a vacant sky and
beckoning us to give it up, to let it go, and
open once again our hearts to one we've hurled outside.

Choice Traps

There are days I feel trapped by my choices,
When the things that I chose no longer seem mine,
But instead seem some burdens that life,
      or the devil,
          or God, if you will,
Have cast on me
      to slow me
          to stop me in my Path
               preventing me from moving forward
               and up into the Light
               to the glorious destiny that is mine.
And yet I know in my heart even then
      that this is not the truth.
      That the things that I have
      and the things I must do
      are the choices I made
once
      or result from them
      naturally.

But on days when my choices seem traps,
This is cold comfort indeed.

Through Others' Eyes

Through others' eyes my life looks different than it does to me.
Others bring a wealth of history, their lives, to viewing mine.
This gives them unique vantage points from which to view
Without attachment and without pain, the symbols I've collected,
Points of reference I can never have.
These are views I never will be clear enough to see.

The knowledge of this difference has been some help at times,
Allowing me to grant just the perspective to my life that,
Coupled with the listener's disposition, gives an engineered
And altered image than that, which in fact, is purest truth,
Creating envy, pity, or delight as might the need arise.
An image not the truth, and not a lie, but both and neither.

Little of me questions this as somehow less than honest
For nothing that I share is without truth, its context merely shifts.
Now I question what I see when I, observer, view another's life.
Is the envy, pity, or delight all engineered? Am I beguiled
Or do I see what's really there? How does my predisposition
Color and add hue to the shadowed outlines of the lives I see?

And so, I think we live apart together on this earth.
We share our lives in ways contrived to leave a false impression.
But we, ourselves, the truth of us, remains too much unknown.
We settle for these poor results and think we've shared our lives.
We live instead apart and too much all alone. And this is sad,
For at our core, who we can share, is only God. Just God.

I'm Angry

I'm angry! Lurid anger drags me down,
A dead and leaden weight that has no life.
A cold and solid plumb of pain it is,
But somehow so tenacious.

I'm angry! Anger tears my soul, each angry thought
Wears me to the bone and hurts no other one but me.
An object of my anger never feels the searing pain I do,
Never suffers from the onslaught of my anguished heart.

I'm angry! Attempts to channel anger into other things
Are doomed. Tortured tracks, pursuits off course,
With no result except the fuming thoughts remembered.
Even danger bares its head, but I don't give a damn!

I'm angry! All the hell with life! And with the one or ones
Who've made me so. I'm angry, pained, and filled with fear.
A scorched and blistered husk of who I really am.
If only I could see right now what will be so clear later.

Later. When I've calmed my mind or my mind has calmed me.
Later. When the storm has passed and I am once again the man
I know within my heart. Later. When the reason for my anger
Will somehow seem so comical, and anger as response the fool's reply.

Later. What of that "later" now, when a hurricane of anger
Controls my sails and tosses me at will? What of that time,
Which always comes, when I'll look back, ashamed of what I've said
And what I've done? What of that now? The hell with that! I'm angry!

Gathering Snow

The boy had traveled from the north.
    From Montreal.
        He lived in Washington, D.C.
        a student there,
        but New York was his home.
And this somehow embarrassed him,
    for he wished to be from anywhere but there.
    That town in New Suburbia with values of the middle class,
        striving to get more,
        and more,
        and more.
    Of what or why he could not understand.

The war in Vietnam was rolling on,
    beginning now its second decade by most reckoning,
And he had traveled to the north at Easter time
    to see if life in Canada would be so bad
    because this war was not his war
    and soon his student life would end.
Within just days of that, he knew,
    the draft board letter would arrive
    to turn his pastel thoughts
    to black and white
    and military green.

So like an army scout he'd gone to reconnoiter
    to see if life as exile could lend him what he sought.
    A peace of sorts.
Little that he saw remains with him,
    except the snow stilled piled high here and there on city streets,
    massive drifts the size of houses even in that April week.
But it is not the Quebec snow that presses down upon him,
    It's other snow and other thoughts and other lasting images.

The roads were clear for his return.
His plan was to drive through New York,
    along the Eastern Seaboard south
    and back to Washington.
And to this end the weather had supported him for some short while.
He'd left the New French city late in the day,
    knowing he would drive all night
    to reach his destination.

But somewhere between Albany
     and other towns on Henry Hudson's river,
     the snow had started.
Slow at first, but gathering,
     speed initially
     and then a great intensity.

The flakes were clumping now.
Together they made massive gobs that tried to settle on the car,
     but fell instead,
     and landed,
     gathering,
     on the highway slipping by below.

Within the hour, moving south,
     he had to slow,
     then slow again to just a crawl,
     the wipers barely able to keep clear the glass so he could see.
     They simply could not sweep away the snow
     that fell between the arcing of the blades.
The car could scarcely move.
And finally it stopped.

The muffled sound of falling snow was like the holding of his breath,
     a pause that quieted his mind
     and stopped the life he knew.
The power and the force of all that silent snow
     was like the cleaning of his short life's slate.
He sat there quietly
     not knowing what to do,
     having no thoughts but simple whiteness
     blank against a dark and leaden midnight sky.
The peace was palpable, and he began to sleep.

The rapping on the window near his ear awoke him with a start.
Sleepily, he peered through windows plastered with a wet and sticky fresco
     and saw the New York Trooper looking with concern for his response.
The boy opened up the door and stepped into the night of falling white.
"The Thruway's closed in both directions, north and south," the trooper said,
"But you can come with me and up ahead about a mile, the restaurant is open.
It's warm, and you can stay until the road is cleared sometime tomorrow."

The boy got in the trooper's car and went with him,
     the only sound
     the squeaking crunch of tire chains
     against the shrouded night.

They did not talk until the boy said, "Thanks," alighting from the car
       to make his way across the drifts of snow
       to the light and warmth
       that glimmered gaily through the restaurant's fogged doors.

Inside, two dozen stranded travelers were scattered here and there.
Truckers who seemed the best of friends were gathered in one booth.
A couple spoke in whispered tones so as not to wake their sleeping children
       sprawled with dangling arms and legs
       on the benches of the booth they occupied.
       A useless act this caution seemed somehow
       amidst the clanking of the dishes
       and the silverware tossed carelessly
       by waitresses in uniforms of pastel pink
       that matched the season but not the night.
       And yet, the children slept.

The boy sat at the counter at one end.
He ordered coffee, warmed his hands in rising steam,
       reviewed the menu,
       ordered eggs and ham and toast,
       this day,
       to his mind,
       just beginning
       rather than the darkest part of yesterday.

The old man with the message came inside and sat down next to him, although
       the counter where they now sat close together offered mostly empty seats.
The cold from outside still surrounded the old man and,
       like an aura,
       radiated from his woolen coat and hat.
       It caused the boy to shiver.
       He drank more coffee from his waiting cup.

"This storm's quite a surprise," the old man said to no one in particular,
       but solely for the boy.
"I guess," the boy replied while looking straight ahead.
"Where you headed?" asked the man.
"To D.C. Back to school," he answered.
"What brings you way up here?" the man asked, honest interest in his voice.
"I live in Montreal," the boy said,
       not seeing where it came from,
       but trying on the lie for size.
       Better than the truth, he thought.
       Yes, better than the truth.
       He glanced outside.

The snow continued falling,
                but he felt warm and snug and safe
                under the blanket of this little lie.
        Yes, better than the truth.

The night dragged on.
The snow continued falling.
Building on itself.
Outside nothing moved except the softly falling whiteness.
Inside, the boy had warmed up to his story.
        Caught up in complexity
        and the risk of telling story upon tale,
        he gathered lies around him like so many cloaks.
        Lies peppered with sufficient truth to keep them somehow real:
        where he'd lived
        and when,
        and what he planned to do with the life
        that stretched before him.
        And he continued,
        feeling safe
        and safer still
        as the blankets of his lies were gathered all around him.
        It was better than the truth,
        he told himself again.
And the old man merely listened, honest interest in his face.

As the cold and leaden morning light spread across the eastern sky,
        the falling snow began to slow,
        and then it stopped.
The boy was tired.
Keeping up the pretense for this long exhausted him in body, mind, and spirit,
        but he felt safe within his refuge of deceit.
        Besides, he justified, the first thing that he'd said had locked him to this course.
        The life he truly owned could never be explained to willing ears.
The old man with the message had said little, listening it seemed to every word.

With the brightening daylight, a different trooper came inside.
He told them that the maintenance crews
        had been on the road for hours.
        The road was mostly clear,
        both north and south,
        and they could all be on their way.

The boy exhaled,
 relaxed,
 relieved,
 knowing his night's labor done,
 and he would now release himself
 from the blanket of the lies he'd gathered,
 release himself from that
 and the old man's interested eyes.

They both got up to leave at the same time,
 the old man heading out to parts unknown,
 the boy not learning even this about him,
 and the boy to trek back to his car a mile away.
 His life would be unchanged,
 in leaving far behind
 this place,
 and the old man
 and his interest.

But the old man then said words he'd keep with him forever,
 in the parting at the door
 came the moment of the message
 in the parting at the door
 came the password to his future,
 the thing the boy had never even known
 he longed to hear.
"I see you are a fine young man," he said,
 "And I am only sorry,
 that in all the time we've spent this night,
 I have not yet met you,
 and that I would have truly wished to do."

Surprise and some embarrassment gathered on the young boy's face,
 but something else began to stir within him
 something new,
 something original,
 something real.
With that, the old man grasped the boy's warm hand,
 and shook it,
 and there was interest in the handshake
 and love the boy was sure,
 and the old man with the message hurried off
 to wherever he had come from
 or would go.

Wrong Turn

The road I should have taken falls behind me to my left.
Headed now for Flagstaff.
    North. The airport to the south.
    My ticket in my pocket. Waiting.

I am not late today. Not time constrained
    Or worried I will miss this plane. Unconcerned,
I look about in certainty. This is my route today, although
    I don't know why this way. Today.

Phoenix towers loom ahead. I see an exit I can take
    Seventh Street.
        An underpass.
            A quick return. And
Back safe on my way.
I take it and pull behind a giant rig that bottoms at the ramp.
    A traffic signal halts us there. I wait to make my left
        And then another up the ramp.
    Returning me to my preplanned but now slight altered route.

And then I see him standing there. Just waiting, too.
    The traffic light controls his life as much as mine right now.
    The ebb and flow of waves of cars whose drivers stop and look.
    Some help. Though most do not.
At the corner, at his crossroads, bearded,
    Clad in dirty clothes. A handsome man. Once.
        Now, one of the homeless.

Some sixty years ago and more,
    When this nation's money system ruptured at its core,
        A "hobo" we'd have said.
But "hobo" is a word of romance meaning
    Trains and cattle cars and
    Better fortune waiting around the bend,
    Widowed matrons granting meals in porcelain kitchens.
        Black and white linoleum tiles. And pies
        Set cooling on broad window sills in sleepy towns.

A different world. Another time. Not now.
No hobo is this man. "Homeless" is his word.
        Descriptive of a generation.
                Turned out from home.
                        Turned out from life.

This homeless man holds his simple hand-scratched sign

                I am hungry

                I am thirsty

                50¢ will help

        It says.

He stares at me in my red rented car. I look at him,
Avert my eyes, look back and see. Not him.
        But me.
                Not me, but us.
                        The all of us together in his eyes.

I am hungry.
        I am thirsty.
                50¢ will help.

I look into my heart and see my willingness to love
Is coated with a film of New Age plastic.
Our eyes connect again and I am falling into Love.
The plastic gone or peeled away. Love rushes through me.
I want to help.
        I have no choice, or rather
                I have chosen.

My wallet right at hand, I look to see what I can do.   Knowing
        It is full.
        I am immensely wealthy when measured by this man
                With much, much more beyond the bills in this thin wallet.

As I power down the window and motion for him to come,
He does, and for a moment, we breathe the same air.
I give him some of what God gave to me.
        It is more than he expects.
                "God bless you!" he cries.
                        "God bless you!"
And I am blessed.